Better

Thinking

Habits

UPCOMING BOOKS BY ADLEY TELFORT

Better Thinking Habits Relationship Edition

Better Thinking Habits Finance Edition

Better Thinking Habits Career Edition

BETTER THINKING HABITS

Introduction Edition

By Adley Telfort

www.adleytelfort.com

ISBN 978-0-9992544-0-0

To Book Author for Speaking Engagements:

To Book author for speaking engagements with corporations, associations, or other organizations. Contact the publisher at the website above.

Printed in the United States of America

Table of Contents

Do you know the difference between a smart person, a clever person, and a wise person?

The smart person learns from their mistakes.

The clever person solves problems.

The wise person avoids problems and mistakes by learning from the mistakes of others.

Better Thinking Habits by Adley Telfort

ACKNOWLEDGEMENTS

Thank you to my mother, Madline Etienne, you are the reason I am the man I am today. If not for you, I don't know where I would be. You are and will always be the most important person in my life.

I love you, mom.

INTRO

The best way to get the things that you want is to become the person who deserves the things that you want.

Better thinking habits: Many people believe that the best way to get ahead in life is to work hard. Many of us spend our entire life working hard and never achieve our goals or even get close to achieving them. The reason for that is because we have poor thinking habits. There's an old saying, "A person is what they think about all day long"—which means, if you're thinking of an idea and you remain focused on it, you'll make it a reality. On the other hand, if you have an idea, but you are focused on things that have nothing to do with that goal, you will never reach it. In fact, your day-to-day actions may be contradictory and may push you further away from achieving your goal. That is why it's important that you evaluate every decision, no matter how big or how small, and determine whether the decision you are about to make is going to help you get closer to your goal or going to push you further away. Taking that one action and applying it to your decision-making process alone can change your life and mindset dramatically. You'll come to find you don't want to hang out at some of the places you did before; you'll stop talking to some of the people you once called friends. You'll start to evaluate everyone and everything around you to see if it or they serve a purpose in getting you closer to your goal.

Whether your goals in life are right or wrong in the eyes of others is not a big concern because it is *your* desire in life. Yes, in the eyes of others, it may seem strange or weird, but to you it's normal. By no means am I saying it's okay to do wrong or illegal things, but what I *am* saying is—this is *your* life, and only *you* know what you can handle, what makes you happy, and what makes you sad.

But here is an essential thing to remember about goals: Goals are nothing but dreams unless you act to make them a reality. Now remember, not all the actions you take to make your dreams a reality will work out in your favor. In fact, you may take some actions that you think will help, but once the action is complete, you may realize, "Holy crap! I just screwed up and pushed myself two steps back from my goal." Things like that will happen during the process of working towards your goals. But one of the key things is to learn from your mistakes and become better.

I believe that for each mistake you *should* beat yourself up a little—but not too much. It is important to learn that whenever you mess up, you should recognize the mistake, find out how and why you did it, then come up with a plan to prevent it from happening again or as few times as possible. You shouldn't beat yourself up to a point where you're in the corner crying and thinking, "OMG! Life is over; I am done. I am a failure; I give up."

Your goals must be something you're passionate about, something you want to do and something you enjoy doing.

Are You A Success?

Many times, people don't even start on their goals, or they quit before reaching them. This is in part due to fear, fear of failure, fear of being laughed at, and sometimes, fear of success. Yes, some people fear reaching their goals. They ask themselves: What if things worked out and I can't handle the stress or workload? That is when you must remember your reason for wanting to reach that goal and let *that* be your driving force.

Take a look at your life; think back to when you were in high school. What were your dreams? What were your goals? Where did you expect to be at this point in your life? Naturally, the goals that you had in high school and college may have changed due to certain situations that may have happened in life.

Would you look at your current situation and say your life has been a success?

Before you can answer that question, you must understand the definition of success. The best description I can find for success is: "The progressive realization of a worthy idea." That is, when a person is working towards a predetermined goal, they don't necessarily have to accomplish or reach that goal to be considered a success as long as they are actively working on it and a time frame is set in place. Success is not measured by materialistic objects or money; success is measured by personal satisfaction and happiness within oneself. The successful person is the man who decides he's going to be a great father, so he goes to work every day, comes home after work, doesn't hang out, doesn't drink, treats his wife with respect, puts his family first. He doesn't have a big house or drive a nice car; his job is hard and pays very little, but his family is happy, and therefore he is a success. If you say that you want something but the things that you're doing are interfering with you reaching that goal, then you are a failure, or you're lying to yourself—the goal you have isn't *really* what you want.

Take Responsibility for Your Life

If you do what's easy, your life is going to be hard. Many people are in relationships where they don't want to argue, so they remain silent. They let the other partner make all the decisions, and many times, that quiet person may end up doing several things they don't enjoy doing. Their life is miserable because they decided to take the easy way out and avoid confrontation. Many of us, when faced with problems in our personal or professional life, like to take the easy way out by blaming everything and everyone around us—from our family members to our circumstances for the cause of our problems—because it is too difficult for us to hold ourselves responsible for our actions. Life is like a movie script—not only are we the writers of that script, but we are also the directors and actors.

If you look at your life, everything that you've got, you made it happen—whether it's good or bad. Directly or indirectly, you made a decision or committed an act that got you to where you are today. The beautiful thing about life is that, at any moment—when you have an epiphany and realize you're unhappy with your current circumstances—you can change it at the snap of your fingers by simply making a decision and committing yourself to that decision to change who you are.

Too often I hear people say, "Change takes time." Nope! It's because they're not ready, are unwilling to change, or fear change. Once you make that decision to change your life by changing your mindset, it will happen. I have a personal belief that when something comes to mind that you know you *should* do, just stop what you're doing and do it with NO EXCUSES.

For example, if you have an argument with your wife first thing in the morning, but now you are at work and you're thinking, "Man, I should call her and apologize. I should get her some flowers." Just stop right there in your tracks, pull out your phone, call her, apologize, buy those flowers, and take them home. Don't sit there and say, "I'll wait till later," because you might forget, or something else may come up. We have to act at that moment. You cannot want something and then not be willing to work for it.

Too often I hear people say, "I want to do this; I should do this." But then, after saying that, they spend the next two weeks or years not doing anything. If you know you made a mistake for example, you should have made a phone call to a family member or friend or reached out to somebody, put the book down and go ahead and call them. If you know you should have enrolled in a class, put the book down and go enroll in the class. Start living your life, start living your goals. If in the next five or ten years you look back at your life and you haven't accomplished anything that you set out to do, you have no one else to blame but yourself—not society, not your parents, not your circumstances, not the government—nobody but yourself.

Be A Leader

There are two types of people in this world. There are leaders, and there are followers. There is no such thing as a natural-born leader; this is either a skill that's acquired at a young age based on our environment, or something that we decide to develop later in adulthood. The truth is that many people are just followers, and they're following behind the ninety-five percent that are unsuccessful. Too many people conform to fit in with society or their environment's idea of what they should be. You should never dress or act based on your current situation. Dress and act as if you are in the place that you want to be in life. Just because you live in the hood, you don't necessarily have to dress and act like everyone else in the hood.

I grew up in a very rough neighborhood, and one of the things that I found incredibly strange was the fact that I would see some of the older men in our community, who in their youth committed crimes or were involved in gang activities, and now, as adults, they're standing in front of corner stores, drinking liquor, without a job, asking people to borrow a dollar, still sleeping at their parents' house, and failing to pay child support for their two or three kids. These grown men with nothing happening for them were the people the young boys in my neighborhood looked up to and wanted to be like. They imitated these men, wearing baggy clothes, having their pants sag. Even as a young child, I realized something: If I followed in those men's footsteps, I was likely going to end up right there with them—in front of the store drinking liquor and asking people to borrow a few dollars, sleeping on my mother's couch, and having kids that I could not support. If more people look at things from that point of view, they will realize that they're following the habits of people who are dependent on someone else for life's necessities.

In life, we need to learn to be students, not followers, and we all should take advice—not orders. Everything done in life should be a product of our conclusions—based on the observation and information that we received. If you're given a piece of advice, process it, and if it makes you wonder and think, then it's valuable; then take action. But make sure the action you take is not what somebody told you. Make sure the action is a product of your conclusion that is based on the advice, observation, and information that you process. Always remember that what works for somebody else may not always work for you.

Live With Purpose

I find that many of us are trapped by dogma. We spend our entire lives living someone else's life, living up to what we think our friends or society expects us to be and never really being ourselves. Take a few minutes and think about this: If you stop doing the things that your friends are doing and start doing some of the things that you really want to do, would you and your friends have anything in common? Would they want to participate in the events you choose? Will they look at you strangely, and will they start to think that you believe you're better than them? Will they start to think that your goals are unreachable and something to be laughed at?

When you think about things like that, it puts things in perspective; it helps you to understand that maybe you're not happy with your current circumstances and the people you hang around with, so you need to make a change. Embrace who you are, embrace your personality, embrace your weirdness. We all are different, we all are unique, and that's what makes this world so special and fun. If we all were alike, it would be a boring world. I have a personal belief that everyone has a purpose in this world, and that's why I try my best not to judge people.

Take for example, if everyone had a college degree. Who would be the garbage people? Who would do the maintenance in the buildings? I'm not saying they're demeaning jobs, but everyone serves a purpose; we all have our role in this world. We all are not meant to be rich, and we're not all intended to be experts in the same area. If that were the case, there would be too much competition and not enough jobs to go around.

Many times, in life, you'll hear people say you can't do something, and that's because they can't do it themselves, so they try to project their inability onto you. Never let somebody else's negativity or bad predictions discourage you in any way. Never believe in a prediction that does not empower you. We all are born with a purpose; there's something that we are supposed to do. When you know you are deliberately living below your capabilities, not trying to grow, not trying to challenge yourself, then you are living a meaningless life. What is your purpose in life? Why are you here? Who's going to miss you when you're gone?

If you haven't touched somebody's life or accomplished anything that would cause people to want to remember you when you're gone, then you're not living; you're just here taking up space. It is necessary that you develop yourself, grow, challenge yourself, and push yourself to the next level to reach your goals. If you have failed at nothing, then you've tried nothing.

Think about it. Do you hate your job? How much time do you spend complaining about how much you hate your job? If so, what have you done about it? What are you going to do about it? Don't just be a clock-watcher, where as soon as it hits that time to punch out, you run out of the workplace; you go home, watch TV, eat something, go to sleep, wake up the next morning, and get ready to do it all over again. That cycle continues for a year, two years, three years, and next thing you know, you've made a career out of that job that you hate. So rather than becoming a clock-watcher, give your current employer one hundred percent. Do your job as if it was your company. At the end of your shift, go home and plan out your goals, so that way you can get out of that job you hate. You must spend time thinking about your goals, how to accomplish them, and doing the things that you need to do to align yourself with them.

Problems Are A Part Of Life

We all have problems, but you cannot be consumed with them; they are part of life. Behind every single problem or stressful situation is an opportunity for you to develop yourself and make yourself a bigger, stronger and better person. Look at a problem for exactly what it is—a problem, something that can be solved. Remember, a situation cannot cause a feeling of anxiety or stress unless we look at the situation and interpret it to be a stressful situation. By doing that, we have caused our own anxiety.

For example, you've been married for the past ten years and have two kids together, but all of a sudden, you find yourself getting a divorce. Is it a bad thing or a good thing? It all depends on your situation and how you look at it. If you came home every night, never spoke to each other, had very little to nothing in common, and slept in the same bed but did not want to touch each other—Guess what! Now you're single. You can go out there and find a person whom you want to be with and who's going to make you happy. What's wrong with that?

Too many times, we focus on what other people are going to say, or how it's going to look, or we focus on the time, money, and energy that we spent creating that relationship, and we tell ourselves, "Now it's all going to waste." The secret to having a happy life is progress. If you look at every single problem or situation that comes up as an opportunity to develop and grow, then you're progressing, and therefore, you'll become happier as you realize that problems *can* be solved. Also, remember any problems you encounter are due to a decision that you made.

It's not about taking a risk; it's always about getting outside your comfort zone, or you will never grow, you will never learn anything, and you will be stagnant. You cannot turn back the hands of time; the only thing you can do is learn from your mistakes and try your best not to make them again.

Three questions you should ask yourself are: Where have you been in your life? What have you done in your life? And where are you going?

The Company You Keep

If you want to see the type of person you are, don't look in the mirror, but look at the company you keep instead.

What kind of people do you surround yourself with? Are you the smartest person in your group? Are you surrounding yourself with "yes sir" or "yes ma'am" people? Are you a "yes ma'am" or "yes sir" person? Are your friends the type of people that would challenge you? Are the people that you surround yourself with the type that will tell you, "Hey, you messed up" when you're wrong, even when they know you need to have them on your side?

You must align yourself with people who have similar goals to yours; this way you learn from each other, encourage each other, and push each other forward. If you're the smartest person in your group, then you need to upgrade and find yourself a set of new friends. The reason for that is because you will find that if your IQ is that of 150, and you're hanging out with people whose IQ is at an 85, then you can never use your full level of intelligence when talking or dealing with these people; therefore, you will dumb yourself down so that they can understand you, and if you continue to do something long enough, it becomes a habit and habits become a part of who you are. That is why you see a lot of intelligent people or people who have great potential messing up in life. They are surrounded by people whom they cannot use their level of intelligence around. Therefore, they are not growing. In fact, they're going in reverse.

Let's go ahead and do a quick test. I would like you to pay close attention to the people that you work with, all the people that are around you. Notice that if you work with somebody who does not speak clear English, who may be from another country with a thick accent, when you speak to that particular person, do you talk slower with an accent and use smaller words because you think that is the only way that person will most likely understand you?

The same concept is true with your friends. If you are at a certain level and your friends are below your level, you will notice that you dummy down your words when speaking with them so that they understand you. If you read the tabloids, you will see that a lot of celebrities are getting themselves into all kinds of trouble, and we sit here wondering, why is it that someone with so much money would do something so stupid or crazy? It just doesn't make any sense. But that's what happens when you are the person in control with the most money in your group and you surround yourself with people who want to make you happy. They agree with anything you say, and they don't open their mouths when you have a stupid or dumb idea to say, "Don't do it." Think about it, you may have a "yes sir/ma'am" person, or you may be that person in the group.

Here's another great example of why we need to have people tell us when we're being dumb or doing stupid things. Think about it, when you are in a relationship and you're upset, or you need somebody to talk to because you have a problem within your relationship, you typically have a group of friends or family members that you may turn to. For me, that is my mother; she is the person that I usually turn to when I have an issue within my relationship, and most of the time, she would sit down and point out to me where I went wrong, or when I was at fault. Very rarely was it my wife or girlfriend's fault when I spoke to my mother, and I came to love that about her. I always knew that before I went off the hinge, I would give my mother a call, talk to her, and find out if I had any reason to be upset, or if it was just me overreacting and being a jerk as most of my exes would call me. Now, thinking about it, if my mother always said, "Baby, you're right, these women are crazy. They don't know what they're talking about," I wouldn't have become the person I am today, and I would continuously make the same mistakes, and when I meet Miss Right, she wouldn't be able to stand my guts because I would think that I'm perfect and she is wrong in every disagreement. We do not need to have "yes sir" people around us, and we need a group of people who will always tell us when we are at fault for our problems.

Life Is A Rollercoaster

Life is always changing; sometimes you're up, sometimes you're down. Some things go well, while sometimes they don't. Sometimes you're happy, sometimes you're sad, but that's life. We must start to accept and understand that happiness, sadness, and hardship are moments that we must all go through in life, but those moments are not here to stay, they are here to pass. Life is opportunity mixed with difficulty.

They Are Who They Are

Stop trying to change people who do not want to change. It is okay to present an opportunity for somebody to better themselves, but if they choose not to better themselves, then let them be. Do not invest your time, energy, and money into trying to help someone who does not want help. You can present opportunities to them and let them make a decision on what they want to do with those opportunities. There's an old saying that goes, "You can lead a horse to water, but you can't force it to drink," and it is the same thing with human beings. It can be hard watching a brother, a sister, a friend, or someone that you care about, go down a path of self-destruction—a path that is going to cause them to harm themselves and the people around them.

I am not saying to let them go down that path, but what am saying is you must explain to them that what they are doing is harmful, and that the most likely outcome as a result of their actions will cause harm, and then you must let them make a decision on whether or not they want to continue down that path. In some cases, they may not care, and they will continue down the destructive path. When you come across people who just don't care, it is vital that you walk away from them. Whether it's a friend, family, or loved one, you must distance yourself from people who don't care to help themselves. If you find yourself getting upset with your partner because they're hanging around certain people who are not good for them, don't get mad at their friends. Remember, your partner is choosing to be around people whom they feel most comfortable with. Look at your friends; you only choose to hang around people who have the same mindset as you, who like the same things as you. In short, do not get upset at people for being who they are. The only thing you can do is present them with the opportunities, point out the things they're doing that can be harmful to their future. Let them make the decision on which path they want to take, and if a loved one is taking a path that is going to cause you harm in the future, you must walk away.

I know it's hard, I know it's tough, I know you don't want to turn your back on a loved one, but the truth of the matter is, we all choose our paths, we all choose which direction we want to go. You cannot be mad and upset with someone for being who they are. If you know someone is a hypocrite and they're being hypocritical, why are you mad at them? They're a hypocrite, and that's what hypocrites do; they're hypocritical.

If someone is a negative person and you know that about this person, why are you getting mad at them when they say negative things? That's who they are, and you're choosing to be around them. If you know your partner is a cheater, then why are you getting mad when they cheat? That's exactly what cheaters do; they cheat. So, don't be angry at someone for doing what's part of their character. Be angry with yourself for allowing that person in your life.

Like the story of the Scorpion and the Frog. The Scorpion comes to a river but can't swim and needs to cross. He sees the Frog, and he asks the Frog for a ride across the river. The Frog says, "No, I can't give you a ride because you're a scorpion; you're going to sting me." The Scorpion says, "Why would I do that? If I sting you when I'm on your back, we both will drown and die." The Frog thinks about it for a minute and says, "It makes sense." So, he decides to give the Scorpion a ride across the river. The Scorpion, halfway through the river, stings the Frog, who feels a sharp pain in his back. The Frog says to the Scorpion, "Why did you sting me? Now we're both going to die." The Scorpion says, "I can't help it. I'm a scorpion, and that's what I do; I sting."

Things You Should Remember

As you grow, the people you associate with will change. Some of your friends will not want you to move on. They will want you to stay at, or below their level. People who don't help you climb are not looking out for your best interest. As you grow, you will notice people in your life who push you forward and the ones who stunt your growth. If someone is not adding value to your life, there is no need for them to be there.

Do not ask or let someone who has no experience or who is in a worse situation than you help you make a decision on how to handle a particular situation. Too often, we turn to friends and family members who are going through the same issues and have not been able to work through it, and we ask them for advice. Taking advice from someone who has made the same mistake repeatedly is the best way to end up with the short end of the stick. Never take or seek advice from someone who has been and still is in the same bad situation as you. (If you have to seek advice from them, just do the complete opposite of what they did). Why discuss your problem with someone who is unable to help solve your issues?

Don't follow someone who is heading nowhere.

It's never too late to walk away from a bad investment. Many times, we invest in things. It can be the stock market; it could be a relationship or friendship, a car, or anything that we believe is of value to us. We have a problem as human beings. We look at the time, at the energy and the money we put into something and feel that person or that thing has taken too much from us, and we need to get something out of it. If you stick to that mentality, you will always end up with the short end of the stick. You may begin investing in something and believing that it is a good investment, but at the end of the day, you then come to realize it's not a good investment. You have to be prepared to walk away no matter how much time, energy, money, or sacrifice you have invested into that object, that thing, or that person. It is better to lose a lot than to lose everything, and yes you will lose *everything* if you continue to invest in a bad investment.

Family will always be family, but you must remember they are human first. And as humans, we are not perfect.

Be honest and stop lying to yourself. If you know that you are a cheater and you get called out for being one, why get upset? Why throw a tantrum? Just accept the fact that you're a cheater. If you know you're a liar, and you get called out for lying, don't get upset; don't get mad especially if you know you got caught in your lie. Too often as human beings, we don't accept responsibility for our character or the things that we do. One of the biggest things you can do in your self-development process is to accept your flaws and your shortcomings. Accept the areas of opportunity that you have, or those that you need to work on.

You must understand how to make decisions; you must weigh the pros and cons as to what you are going to gain and lose if you were to decide to do something. Now, which one holds the greater weight, the pros or cons? If you apply this thinking habit to every decision that you make, you'll find yourself always ending up with the longer end of the stick.

In this day and age, no matter what type of job you have, you can afford nearly anything you want through financing, but you must ask yourself this one question: "You can afford to buy it, but can you afford to keep it? You can afford to buy a $300,000 house with $30,000 down payment, but can you afford the mortgage? You can afford to buy a $40,000 car with $8,000 down payment, but can you afford the maintenance? You can afford just about anything you want with a good credit and a down payment, but can you afford to keep it?

When investing your finances, the worst possible place to invest your money is in a vehicle; the minute you drive that vehicle off the lot, it depreciates. Why spend thousands of dollars on a vehicle to look good if it serves no purpose? The worst thing you can do is look like you have money, drive a nice car and not have a penny to put gas in the tank.

The best revenge you can ever have if somebody cheats on you is by not doing the same. Don't cry if your partner cheats on you, let them go. Then, work on yourself. You will become better and more successful, and you'll make sure that the next relationship is something that is going to flourish and be beautiful. The next time your ex-partner sees you, they will say, "Oh my gosh, what a beautiful person. I missed out on that opportunity. Holy crap."

If somebody tells you that you're not going to succeed in life, don't argue and fight with them. Prove them wrong. Work your behind off to become ten times more successful than you were at the time when they spoke to you. This way, the next time that person sees you, they'll be asking *you* for a job.

Whenever a friend or someone you hold dear turns on you, stabbing you in the back, you cannot be mad at them; you must be angry with yourself. You allowed this person to be in your life, so *you* are responsible for the consequences or anything that happens as a result and no one else. There—more than likely—were signs that this person was capable of what they did.

When things are good for you, your family and friends will know you. When things are bad for you, you will know who your true family and friends are. You should always be there for the ones you love, regardless of if things are good or things are bad, as long as they want and are willing to help themselves.

Any behaviors you accept in your loved ones are the same behaviors you will adopt because you see nothing wrong with what they are doing.

Stay Focused On Your Goal

Short Story

A person has decided that their goal is to purchase a new vehicle in the next six months, and they decide to pick up overtime hours at work and perhaps start a second part-time job to get that vehicle within the set timeframe. Now, this person has set a goal, has set up the parameters for meeting that goal, and is now on his or her way to achievement. One month into working towards the goal, this person is working an average of ninety hours every two weeks at their full-time job. They also picked up an extra twenty hours at their new part-time job, giving them an average of one hundred and ten hours of work every two weeks. It's now month two, and this person starts thinking, "I'm working so hard; I haven't had a day off; I'm working all these hours and need to start treating myself. This weekend, I'm going to go out to the spa and have a very relaxing day. I deserve it." Another two weeks pass by, and the person says, "I've been working so hard with no days off; I need to treat myself. I'm going to go buy some new clothes." Two weeks after that, the person says, "I've been working so hard that I haven't had the chance to enjoy myself, so I'm going to go out to eat this weekend and have drinks with friends."

Before you know it, the sixth month has arrived and the person has hardly any money saved because their focus shifted from their goals to "I am working so hard, I need to treat myself."

Lesson to Learn

It is so easy for us to become sidetracked when working towards our goals; this is why we must have better-thinking habits to keep the focus on our goals.

Your Clothing Is Your Uniform

Short Story

A man is walking down the street when suddenly he is attacked from behind by a bandit wearing a ski mask and holding a knife. "Give me your wallet!" the robber demands. And the poor and hopeless victim hands over his wallet. The victim, unsure if he would make it home to his family, then sees a man in a police uniform walking toward him, texting on his phone and unaware of the robbery happening in front of him. "Help! Help me!" yells the poor victim. It is at this time that the man in the police uniform looks up and notices what is happening less than ten feet in front of him, so he quickly and without hesitation turns around and runs the other way. Later that night, the man in the police uniform while having dinner with his wife tells her what happened earlier that morning with the bandit in the ski mask and the victim being robbed. His wife then replies, "You did the right thing, honey. How dare people automatically assume you are a police officer just because you're wearing a police officer uniform."

Lesson to Learn

Our clothing is our uniform. Perception is reality. If you dress in a policeman's uniform, then people will assume you are a police officer. It can also be said that if you dress like a thug, then you will—more than likely—be treated like one. If you dress like an escort, you will—most likely—be addressed like an escort. Dress like a businessman, and you—more than likely—will be treated with respect. Dress like a lady, and—more than likely—you will be treated like a lady. Notice the use of the words "more than likely"—which means there is a greater chance that something will happen (but it is not always guaranteed to happen).

What Would You Do?

It is two o'clock in the afternoon; you are home alone, and your doorbell rings. When you look out the window, there is a man standing at your front door. His jeans are sagging and exposing his boxers; he has tattoos covering his arm and neck. When he notices you at the window, he states, "I'm here to complete your tax return." It was at this time you remembered that you had signed a request to have a representative from the IRS stop by your home to help you complete your taxes. Would you open the door, let this person into your home, and give them all your personal information?

On Your Death Bed

Short Story

At 3:45 p.m., a man was lying in his hospital bed in deep thought, but his mind was at peace—for today he would die. He had placed all his affairs in order and said his goodbyes to loved ones. "Are you ready?" asked the doctor.

The man lying in bed nodded his head. "Yes, doctor, I'm ready."

As the doctor proceeded to inject the IV tube, he stated to the man in the bed, "This will put you to sleep, making your transition painless."

As the man in the bed slipped into a deep sleep, he was suddenly awakened by a sense of unease—as if he was surrounded by danger. As he looked up from his bed, he saw that the room was filled with familiar faces that he knew but could not remember who they were or how he knew them. The one thing that he knew for sure was that not one face in that room was happy to be there or wanted to be there. "Who are you and what do you want?" stated the man in the bed.

One of the faces stepped forward and into the light. "We are the dreams and ideas that came to you in life hoping you would bring us to life. WE CAME TO YOU, AND IT WAS ONLY YOU WHO COULD HAVE BOUGHT US TO LIFE, NOW WE ARE FORCED TO DIE WITH YOU."

The man than felt a hand touch his left shoulder and a voice said, "I was the book you never wrote," Another voice said, "I was the trips you never took." Another voice yelled, "I was that business you never started!"

As if it was a perfectly coordinated recital, each face stepped forward listing which unfilled dream or idea they were. The doctor unplugged the life support machine, and the coroner ruled time of death as four p.m.

Lesson to Learn

Don't let your dreams and ideas die with you. If an idea comes to you, it came to you for a reason. It is your duty to try and make it come true. You only have one life to live, so why not live a meaningful and purposeful life.

What Would You Do

If your doctor told you that you had only three months to live, what things would you do before you die? Where would you travel to before you die? Who would you visit before you die? What relationships would you fix before you die? What foods would you eat before you die? Who would you want to spend your last three months on this earth with?

This is how you should view life. Live every moment like it is your last moment on Earth but don't be reckless and stupid. I REPEAT: This is not an endorsement to be reckless and stupid with your life. I repeat, no YOLO.

The Cup Half Full or Half Empty

Short Story

It is noon, and a lawyer is preparing to meet with a client. At 12:15 p.m., the lawyer walks into the conference room, and sitting there across from him is a potential new client whose spirit seems broken, and you can see that they have been in a state of depression for some time now.

"So why are you here today?" asked the lawyer.

"I would like to get some information on filing bankruptcy," said the person sitting across from the lawyer.

The lawyer, sensing this person's feelings of hopelessness, began to give the same speech that he has given to countless other clients. "Bankruptcy can be viewed from two different points of views; one view is that you mismanaged your money, we're irresponsible, couldn't handle all the bills you created over the years, and now you have to file bankruptcy and start over. The other point of view would be that you mismanaged your money; yes, you were irresponsible and couldn't handle all the bills you created over the years, but now you can get rid of those bills without having to pay them. You get a new start; it would be like hitting the do-over button."

The potential client smiled and said, "I never looked at it from that point of view, when can we file the paperwork."

Lesson to Learn

Like anything in life, a situation, even one like bankruptcy, can never cause sadness, anger, depression, happiness, anxiety, or a feeling of any kind until your brain sees the situation then produces an interpretation of that situation and you believe that interpretation to be true. If you interpret a situation as being sad, you'll become sad. If you understand that same situation to be good, you'll become happy. You control your feelings; your feelings have no control over you.

Be A Leader Not A Follower

Short Story

At a job fair sat this young twenty-three-year-old man, waiting to be interviewed for a job. Two hours had passed and finally the twenty-three-year-old man was called in front of the hiring manager. "Currently, we only have stock room positions available. That position includes unloading trucks every day and pulling pallets full of merchandise to the sales floor. It's a very labor-intensive job, and it pays seven dollars and fifty cents per hour. Do you want the position?"

"Yes," said the twenty-three-year-old man. Later that night, the twenty-three-year-old man was sitting at home, angry and mad at himself, thinking, *Why did I take this job? Is this going to be it for me because I have no college degree?*

The first day of orientation, he sat in a room full of people—old and young, who looked as if they had worked labor jobs their entire life and were barely getting through life. Suddenly, the store manager came to the front of the room and introduced himself. "I started with this company ten years ago as a bagger making six dollars and fifty cents an hour; now I am a store manager making over one hundred thousand dollars a year. This company offers some great opportunities as an hourly associate. You can be promoted every six months. If you become a salary manager, you can apply for promotions every year. When I started as a bagger, I knew that wasn't what I wanted to do for the rest of my life, but I needed money, had no work experience or a college degree, so I had to make do with what I had. I came to work on time every day, asked to be cross trained in different areas, and eventually, I became a cashier, then a lead cashier and continued to get promoted after that. Within three years, I was making fifty-six thousand dollars a year as an assistant manager. Each one of you can do the same."

Suddenly the twenty-three-year-old man was inspired.

Lesson to Learn

You can have more then you've got because you can become more than you are. Never let your current status or job define who you are or where you can go.

The Family Man

Short Story

There once was a lady, who was going through a rough time in her relationship. The man she spent half her life with broke up with her. Her parents, family, and friends were all upset because they felt as if this man had played with her heart. They said to her, "You should never speak to him again. You should move on with your life and start seeing other people. That guy doesn't love you. If he did, he wouldn't have left you." Without a second thought, she agreed.

Now, five years have passed, and the lady finds herself at the age of forty-three still single and dating, while the guy has moved on with his life and became very successful. One day, while she was hanging out with her family and friends, they said to her, "How is it that you let that guy go? He loved you; he gave up a lot to be with you; he provided, never cheated, never hit you; he's very smart; you got nearly everything you wanted; that guy's whole life revolved around you and the kids. What happened? Why did things not work out?"

She thought for a moment and said, "But you guys were the ones who told me to leave. Not one of you said, 'He loves me; he gave up a lot to be with me; he's a provider; he never cheated; he never hit me; he's very smart; he gives me nearly everything I want; that his whole life revolved around the kids and me.' Not one of you guys told me that I needed to save my relationship and that I had a good man."

Lesson to Learn

When you have a problem in your relationship, the one person you need to discuss it with is your partner. Most of the time, family and friends are the ones who give you the worst advice because they don't want to tell you the truth, especially when you're the one in the wrong. (They just want to be supportive and don't mean any harm.) Stop looking for approval outside your relationship, and keep people out of your business.

Be Loyal To Country, Not Your Political Party

To grow and develop yourself, you must be willing to adapt and learn from other people, whether it's your enemy or your best friend. When it comes to political parties, we have Republicans, and we have Democrats. Should we be confined to the sole beliefs of Democrats or the sole beliefs of Republicans? Wouldn't it make more sense to pick and choose the good from each group and bring it together? If you are a Democrat and the Republicans, come out with a great bill, why not support it? If Democrats come out with a great bill that you believe in and you are Republican, why not support that particular bill? Just because you support that particular bill does not make you a traitor, it does not make you less Republican but a better American. Choose something that's going to help the country regardless of who came up with the idea. We've got to get rid of this idea of being loyal to our party; you may agree with ninety percent of your party's ideas, but if another party has that other ten percent that you agree with, why not agree with them on that ten percent and agree with your party on the other ninety percent.

The Double Standard

People always say there's a double standard when it comes to women and men. A man can sleep with all the women he wants and not be judged, and that's not correct. A woman can sleep with all the men that she wants, and she will be judged just as a man is judged. What both sides must understand is that once a man decides to be a player, sleeping with multiple women, he is making a decision to bypass or take the chance of missing the right person.

It is the same thing with a woman. If she's sleeping with multiple partners, she may meet the right guy, but because her focus is not on a long-term relationship, she may miss out on that opportunity. This is why many men and women who decided to live that lifestyle end up old and alone; and there's nothing wrong with that if that's the lifestyle that they chose.

Another thing that people who decide to live that lifestyle must understand is that when they do meet the right person and want to settle down, trust is always going to be a big problem. Their partners will not feel as if they can trust them because of their past. You cannot use the argument that if a person loves you, then they should not be judging your past. We all must be judged based on our past. You cannot expect to create a future with a person if you don't look at their past. You've got to look at their former actions so you can know what to expect in the future.

Our history gives an idea of where a person is going in the future. So, my answer to that is, yes, a woman can do the same thing a man does, she has just got to be willing to accept the consequences of her decisions. Good women would not normally marry a guy that sleeps around, and a good man would normally not marry a woman that is promiscuous.

It's Not What You Say; It's How You Say It

Regardless of if it's an argument or disagreement that you have with your partner, always be careful of the words you use and how you use them. If you and your partner were having a discussion and your partner says: "I'm going to have dinner with my ex from college, what do you think?" Compared that statement to: "My ex from college is in town, and they wanted to know if I can have dinner with them. What do you think?"

Can you figure out the difference between the two? In the first paragraph, the person already said: "I'm going to have dinner with my ex. What do you think?" There's nothing to think about if you've already made your decision that you're going to go based on how you expressed the sentence. Now, when you approach your partner and say: "My ex is in town, and they would like me to have dinner with them. What do you think?" Now, you're asking for feedback because you haven't made a decision. Big difference. Words are very powerful, and it's not *what* you say, it's *how* you say it.

Keeping Your Relationship Fresh

Regardless of if you're a man or woman, we tend to get very comfortable in our relationships after a period of time, but we must understand that a relationship is like a job, and you must always be striving for the next level. If you get complacent in your actions or your habits, your relationship is going to become boring, and somebody is going to start wandering off. All it would take is someone coming in and telling that partner of yours, "Hey, you're beautiful; I appreciate you; you're smart; I like your hair," and because you're not doing those things, your partner may leave.

Always remember you must set the bar high; the higher you set the bar the harder it is for anybody else to come in and create disruption in your relationship. If you do not set the bar high and you become complacent, that is when you open the door for somebody else to come in and take your place. If you believe that if that person allows someone else in, then they never really loved you, rethink it. No, it's just that *you* stopped loving, *you* stopped making them feel loved, *you* stopped making them feel wanted. We all want to feel loved, and we all want to feel wanted. Nobody intends to be the person that's ignored and not treated right. We all want to be with someone who makes us feel wanted, and if you stop making your partner feel that way, it's just human nature that their eyes will start to wander. If somebody else comes in and catches your attention and makes you feel special, you're going to go that route, and nobody stays with someone who doesn't make them feel loved.

Crab Bucket Syndrome

When a single crab is put into a lidless bucket, they surely can, and will, escape. However, when more than one crab is in a bucket, none can get out. If one crab elevates himself above the others, they will grab this crab and drag it back down to share the mutual fate of the group. The term "crab mentality" is used to describe a kind of selfish, short-sighted thinking that runs along the lines of: "If I can't have it, neither can you." Crab bucket syndrome is often used to describe social situations where one person is trying to better themselves and others in the community attempt to pull them back down. People who are trying to get out of bad life situations often find themselves foiled by friends and family members who keep sucking them back in. So, what it comes down to is that you cannot be envious of somebody you love. If you care for a person, you should rejoice in the news with them, and whenever they are trying to accomplish something, you should be willing to help them in whatever capacity you can.

Is Your Character In Line With Your Goals?

Is your character in line with your goals? To understand what that means, you must first understand what a goal is. A goal is anything that you want and that you're working towards. Whether it's by being a good housewife, being a good mother, having a loving relationship, or going to school to become a doctor or lawyer. Whether it's to buy that car you want or having a good paying job to take care of your family. A goal is anything that you want and that you are working to get. That is a goal.

How many of us want to be in a loving and committed relationship? There is no way you can say that and post half-nude photos of yourself, thinking it will not affect your chances of finding a good man who will respect you.

There's no way you can sit there and say that you want people to start looking at you as a businessperson when you're walking around with your pants sagging off your butt with your underwear exposed.

Is your character in line with your goals? Do you want to become the greatest basketball player of all time? How are you going to be able to do that if you don't want to practice?

Do you want to have a good man who is going to respect you and treat you right? How do you expect to find him if you're always in the clubs, posting videos on Facebook of you shaking your hips and twerking for everybody to see.

How do you hope to raise your daughter to be a young lady and not get pregnant while in middle school or high school if you're buying her little shorts with her booty hanging out when she is young. As she grows up, let say you continuously buy these things which exploit her sexuality, then when she's having sex at the age of twelve or thirteen, you will ask how this happened.

Ladies and gentlemen, you must think of your goals and think of the things that you need to do to make your goals happen. If you want something, then you have to be willing to do whatever you need to do. Your goals must be in line with your character—otherwise you will never reach them.

Picking The Right Relationship Partner

As a young man, I was raised by a single mother, and she was determined not to have me turn out like my brothers, who are womanizers. As I became an adult, I would see one woman one week, and another the next. It got to a point where I became a serial dater. My mother became very upset with that and thought that I was a womanizer, sleeping with these women and just moving on to the next. That's when I told my mother: "Mom, you did a much better job than you thought raising me. I can go on a date with a woman, and typically, by the end of the first date, I know whether or not this relationship will be going anywhere. If I notice that our date is not going anywhere, I just call it quits and not waste her time as well as mine with another date."

Too many times, I find people are afraid to be honest and straightforward on the first date. Everyone wants to put on a mask and pretend to be somebody or something that they are not.

I believe that is where the problem lays. So, for those of you out there that are still single or dating, here are a few tips on how to find the right person to spend the rest of your life with.

Ladies, if you are dating a guy, you may want to go out and have lunch or dinner on the beach. Now, as you're sitting there at your table outside, people watching, if you notice that he is breaking his neck and looking at every woman that passes by in a two-piece bikini while you're sitting there in front of him, this shows you that this man has no self-control and that lust drives him.

This rule applies to both male and female. When you sit down, and you ask that person that you're on a date with, "Where do you see yourself five to ten years from now?" They'll likely say something such as they plan on owning their own business or something similar. It is at this point where you hit them with the follow-up question: "What exactly are you doing right now to work toward that goal?" If you got a blank stare, or they completely go around the question and do not answer it, then you know that person is full of it, and at that point you get up and walk away.

Another situation that goes both ways: Check out the person's social media page, and if you notice that the guy likes pictures of half-naked women and that he is mainly following women who seem to be strippers or YouTube video twerkers, then you know lust drives him. If you look at a lady's Facebook page, and every weekend, she's out partying with friends, having drinks and wearing skimpy outfits, but she has two kids at home, yet her profile bio states, "loving mother of two looking for serious relationship". This is somebody whom you should run from. They're saying one thing, but their actions are saying something else.

If you notice that the guy is driving a nice car and has nice clothes but still stays at home with his mom, then you need to leave; his priorities are completely messed up. The money he spent on the down payment for his car could have been devoted to getting an apartment or house.

Too many times I'll see a woman dating a man who already has three baby mamas, who is not supporting his kids, and they think he's going to have a child with them and things will be different. They believe he's going to stay and support that child. If he did not stay with the first three, what makes you think he's going to stay with you and support the child?

Looking at a person's friends are good indicators of what to expect or what kind of person you are dealing with. If you notice that a guy has a bunch of friends who are not doing anything with their lives and always chasing women, then why is he hanging with them if they have nothing in common?

If you noticed that a female, you're talking to has friends that are always partying, hanging out and having relations with different men, if she has nothing in common with them, then why is she hanging with them.

One of the most important indicators is how a person interacts with his or her parents. If there is no respect for the parents, then there will be no respect for you. The parents are the ones who brought them into this world, and you're just someone whom they met here. I believe that regardless of the circumstances, a person should always have a level of respect for their parents; they may not want to deal with them, but they will not disrespect them.

So, if you take these few things and you put them all together, it will give you an excellent indication of the type of person you're dealing with.

Being Better Parents

I recently read an article on a Good Samaritan who was walking past a Dollar Store. Inside the store, he noticed that an armed robber was holding the employees at gunpoint. He pulled out his weapon and asked the robber to put the gun down and not to move. As the thief turns around with gun still in hand, the Good Samaritan shoots the robber, injuring him and saving the lives of the employees. But this robber's family did an interview, and their response to what happened was: If the Good Samaritan saw that their family member was robbing the store, the Good Samaritan should have mind his own business. So, the family is condoning the violent actions of their loved one, basically saying, "If you see our family members doing anything wrong, just mind your business, let them kill and rob whomever they want. As long as your life is not in immediate danger, just mind your business."

That mindset is why this young man was out there robbing stores at gunpoint. He knows at the end of the day, regardless of what he does, his family is going to support his actions.

Bad Spending Habits

We all have our little guilty pleasures. My girlfriend, in particular, loves shoes. There is nothing wrong with buying things that you like whether it's expensive or cost-efficient. The key to having a good healthy bank account is living within your means. If you work at Wal-Mart and you make nine dollars an hour, you're going to drive a nine-dollar-an-hour car, you are going to have a nine-dollar-an-hour closet, and you will have a nine-dollar-an-hour lifestyle. There's no way you can be working making nine dollars an hour but living the lifestyle of somebody who's making one hundred thousand dollars a year. You cannot be driving a forty-thousand-dollar luxury vehicle. Well, let me rephrase that: yes, you can afford to buy a car by financing of course, but can you keep that luxury vehicle if something goes wrong with it?— take, for example, the 2002 Jaguar S-Type: the replacement of a fan on that vehicle brand new is going to be about twelve hundred dollars, and for it used, you're looking at about eight hundred dollars. How long would it take you to save the money for the part after paying all your bills with a nine-dollar-an-hour job?

Too many times have I been in my car driving by the bus stop, and I'll see somebody standing there with a pair of Beats By Dre headphones on. Those headphones can run anywhere between one hundred dollars and up, but yet you're catching the bus, and not only that but the person is also wearing a hundred-dollar-plus shoes.

These are spending habits that will keep you broke. If you continuously spend money on material things that lose value the moment you walk out the store with them, you will never have money. You must look at every purchase that you make as an investment. I walk around with a Blu cell phone, which is a local Miami company, and my cell phone does everything that a Samsung Android or an iPhone would probably do. It only cost me $125, why would anybody spend hundreds of dollars more on the phone just to make phone calls or surf the web? If I spend that kind of money on the phone, it's got to serve a purpose. I most definitely will be using ninety percent of the functions of that phone. Most people who have the Samsung or the iPhone barely use ten percent of the phone's true capability.

Here is another spending habit that will keep you broke. For some time I worked as a lending officer. Too many times people will come in my office and use their cars as collateral to secure a loan. The car is paid off and in some cases the vehicles are two or three years old, that means they saved up to $15,000 or more to buy a car in cash and don't own a house. Every purchase that you spend your money on, you must look at it as an investment. How does it benefit you, and what is it going to be worth once you're done with it?

Stop Embracing Negative Stereotypes

This generation is so messed up it seems it has simply decided to throw out all the things that make a civilization civilized. The women are twerking all over the place in front of their kids, wearing nothing but booty shorts and getting butt injections. Not caring if a man is attracted to them mentally or emotionally, they only want that physical attraction.

It has gotten to a point where men are no longer working, and women are working and taking care of the man; the men are cheating and treating a woman with no respect. If a lady meets a good man who has a good job and carries himself well, it seems he's too much of a nice guy. But the guy walking down the street with his pants sagging off his behind, looking at every woman that passes by him with lust in his eyes is the one that gets the girl.

Women are now embracing being cheated on. Check social media: there are tons of videos of women beating up the side chick and staying with the cheating man. In many cases these are the same men that are beating them and calling them all types of names.

I've looked and very rarely do I ever find a man who holds open a door for a woman.

When a woman walks out on the streets, she is a reflection of her man, and what she does reflects on him and what he does reflects on her. Today's women take pride in having multiple guys around saying, "Well, if a man can do it, then why can't I?"

Too many times do you see the videos posted online, where parents are having sex in front of the kids or having sex so loud the kids hear them. These are things that must end with this generation, or all hope is lost for future generations to come.

Relationship Warning Signs

While many relationships may display one or two of the signs listed below, a toxic relationship will often feature many of these signs, which should be an alarm bell.

Signs of a toxic relationship include: you never turning to each other for emotional support. You look to other people first. Your partner implies that you are stupid, or that they are "the smart one" in the relationship; they try to dissuade you from trying something new because "you probably won't understand it." Your partner implies that they only value you for one thing, whether it be sex, your looks, or your ability to earn money. You can't identify any ways you've positively influenced each other. For example, you haven't adopted any of each other's interests or taught each other any new skills. You can identify ways you've negatively influenced each other, particularly harmful habits like heavy drinking, laziness, or smoking. Your partner is dismissive of your emotions. You don't feel you're able to get your partner's attention when you want to talk about something important. When you're not physically together, it feels like "out of sight, out of mind." Stonewalling. You or your partner flat-out refuse to talk about some important relationship topics. You catch your partner lying repeatedly.

Food For Thought

We can typically tell by the second date if a person is the right one or not, always remember you must place a value on yourself and your time. If you're looking for a lifetime partner and you don't feel like that person is it, then just leave. You can lose money and make it back, you can lose a home and replace it, but your time, once lost, is gone for good; you can't replace it or get that time back.

Which Beast Are You Feeding

There is an old Native American story that explains a battle that goes on in every human being. The battle is between two beasts. One beast is vain, hard-headed, bitter, and full of envy and anger. The other beast is humble, compassionate, courageous, understanding, and full of joy and empathy. Of the two beasts, which one is likely to win? The answer is whichever one you feed the most.

Think about your daily routine and interactions. What shows do you watch? Who do you associate with? What type of music do you listen to? What books do you read? What type of conversation do you have? These are the things that feed the beast within each of us.

If you are always angry and hang around negative people, then you are feeding the negative-angry beast within you. Like anything in life, the more it eats, the stronger it gets; eventually, that beast will take over, and that is who you will become.

Waiting On That Perfect Time To Do Something

There will never be a time in your life when it's the perfect time to do something. If you're waiting for the perfect moment or that perfect timing, it may never come. It is up to you to create that perfect time or the perfect moment. You'll never reach your goal unless you put in the work. The change will not come if you wait for some other person or that perfect time to make it happen.

Get Out Of Your Comfort Zone

A lot of people become comfortable with their lives. They stop growing; they stop wanting more out of life; they become satisfied—not because they have all they want, but because what they got is all they believe they can have in life. Do you think you are settling, or are you working towards something?

Always Be Willing To Learn

There are many things you may think you don't need to know, but having that knowledge may one day be useful and save your life, your career, or help a loved one. So always be open to learning new things.

Don't Expect People To See Your Visions

Whatever goal or dream is given to you is yours, and no one may see what it is you see. So you cannot expect other people to be as excited or passionate about your goals as you are.

You Can't Help Everyone

We all know people who have great potential, but they do nothing with that potential. You can't beg or force people to reach their full potential. As the old saying goes: You can't help someone who doesn't want to help themselves.

You're Where You Are In Life Because Of You

If you're not where you want to be in life, if you don't have what you want in life, or if you are not where you think you should be at this time in your life, it has nothing to do with anyone or anything else, it has everything to do with *you*. Your decision making got you where you are as of right now.

Whose Goal Are You Helping To Accomplish

If you have no goals or have a goal and are not working towards it, you will end up working for someone and helping *them* to make *their* goal a reality.

Don't Live For Other People

Don't live for other people, live for you—so that one day, if a loved one needs you, you're going to be in a position to help them out. If you live for others, you may be so busy helping them that you may never reach your full potential.

You Can Change Your Circumstances

One of the great things about life is that you can get more than you have if you decide to become more than you are. Unless you change who you are, you will continue to have what you got.

You Let You Down

When things around you are falling apart, you have no one to blame but yourself. You made decisions that led up to this moment. Always remember, you can only control *your* actions, not the actions of others.

Stop With The Tit For Tat

If someone is upset with you and they are yelling, and you start to yell back, you will end up in a yelling match, and no one's point will get across.

Never Get Too Comfortable

To become successful, you must work very hard; to stay successful you must continue to work hard. So in other words, to keep what you have, you must keep doing what you did to get what you got.

How Do You Handle Failure

Failure is not the end, but choosing to continue after you fail is what's important. (Remember, when you fail, it's a learning experience to prepare you for round two, three etc..) Be thankful for hard times; they only make you stronger. Don't let failure kill your drive, and don't let success go to your head.

How Do You View Life

If you find out your partner is cheating on you and has been doing so for more than a year, shouldn't you leave them and be thankful they didn't give you an STD? Look at every situation as the glass is half full. You can focus on the fact that the glass is half full or that the glass is half empty. Be open and positive enough to see opportunities. The problem is not the problem; the problem is your attitude towards the problem.

Logic Versus Imagination

Logic can ensure you complete what you have to do in a safe and controlled way without taking on too much risk. Your imagination will push you past your logic to try or accomplish extraordinary things. Only those who risk going too far can find out how far they can go. You can't be too careful, but you can't be too reckless.

Follow Your Intuition

When you come to a crossroad in your life—it can be about your job, relationship, or family—always follow your intuition; it somehow knows actually what you want.

What Determines Our Future

Your future is determined by the action you take today, tomorrow, and the day after. If your future looks bad and you wish to change it, start making better decisions today.

Being Great Isn't Easy

Doing anything great will not be easy, and if you give up, you're not worthy of greatness.

Don't Fool Yourself

If you tell a lie and you tell it enough times, you'll start to believe your lies.

Choose Your Position Carefully

Many times we choose to put our foot down and stand our ground—only to find we are in the wrong. So think before you act or speak, and always be willing to change your position if need be.

You're Not Perfect

If enough people are telling you the same thing, then maybe, just maybe, you should listen. After all, no one's perfect.

Actions Speak Louder Than Words

Don't judge anyone by what they say—words are too easy to speak—judge them by what they *do*. Actions are harder to accomplish. Don't be wise in words, be wise in deeds.

How to Destroy Your Enemy

If you fight with the enemy, they live to fight another day. If you kill your enemy, you go to jail. But if you make your enemy your friend, you now have an ally.

How to Look at Failure

You have not failed, you just learned how not to do something. You can only become smarter if you learn from your mistakes.

Your Character Says What?

Look around you, if you pay close attention, you will notice how people interact with you. Some show respect, some disgust, some fear. Now pay attention to the behavior you display around each person, which may have created the way they interact with you.

Don't Waste Time

We all are quick to say we love life, but we waste so much time, and that is what life is made of: TIME. Begin on your goals, because *later* sometimes becomes *never*. We have the same twenty-four hours, three hundred sixty-five days of the year as the richest people on earth; the key difference is how they use their time and how we use ours.

Circumstance Versus Opportunity

Circumstance is something that happened due to conditions beyond your control. Opportunity is something that happened because you created the conditions for it. So there is no excuse for your lack of opportunity.

How You View Yourself

If you are unable to accept or consider other people's perspective what does that say about you? No matter how right you think or feel you are, always be willing to listen and learn better ways.

Missed Chances

You have failed at every opportunity you decided not to go after, don't be afraid of failure; be afraid of not trying.

Stop Waiting

Stop waiting for change. Stop waiting for inspiration. Be the change and the inspiration you're waiting on.

How Change Starts

Everyone thinks of changing their situation, but it's not the situation that needs changing. You must first start by changing your mindset and attitude; otherwise, you will end up back there again because you kept the same decision-making process.

We Are Not Born Experts

The first time you try something, the odds are that you will not do it right because it's your first time; you're an amateur at it. So don't be scared to try new things and look like a fool in the process. When you fail at something, it's an opportunity to begin again—this time more intelligently—because you learned from your failed attempt.

Be Thankful for what you have.

Do not spoil what you have by focusing on what you don't have. Always remember that what you have now is something you once hoped you had.

Knowledge Is Power

If you look at any major corporation, there is always one person that they select to be the CEO or president. This individual must have the knowledge to run an organization. Look at your group of friends; there is always that one person, the most knowledgeable one, that everyone turns to when they need help. The more knowledge you have, the more power you gain in your personal and professional life.

Who Are You Following

An army of fools led by a General can out beat an army of generals led by a fool any day. Be careful not to follow a fool.

Prove Them Wrong

You should take great pleasure in doing things that people tell you are beyond your reach; use their negativity as fuel to drive you forward so that later on you can rub it in their face.

Pain Builds Character

No matter how hard you try to hide your troubles, people will see, and they will talk about you. The same individuals will also notice how you change once you overcome your difficulties.

Turn Your Weakness to Strength

We all have weakness/areas of opportunity. It's by identifying that area of opportunity, admitting it's a weakness, then working at it can you turn that weakness into strength.

Invest in the Goose, Not the Egg

If you are given a choice to pick either the goose that lays the golden eggs or one golden egg, most of you would choose the goose that lays the golden eggs. But when it comes to the real world, I see that people are investing in the one golden egg, and not the goose that laid it. Let me explain: the egg is anything materialized that loses value the minute you walk out the store with it. These things could be your car, clothing, jewelry, big screen TV, boat, bedroom set, cell phones, etc. The goose would be anything that brings in money or adds value; these things could be an education, starting a business, long- or short-term investments, stocks, self-development, a 401k plan, etc. Now, evaluate your assets. Are you investing in the goose that lays the golden eggs or the one golden egg?

Don't Let Fear Win

In the planning stage of any project, you have to evaluate all possible outcomes, either good or bad. But you must learn to recognize illusions from reality. Don't let your fear of what could happen (worst possible outcome) prevent you from trying if the reward outweighs the risk.

Learn from the Failures of Others

If you want to learn something very quickly, just talk to someone who has tried it and failed, then do the exact opposite of what they did. A wise person learns from the mistakes of others.

Let Them Talk

Don't get upset and want to fight or argue with someone because they're talking about you. That is usually a sign that they're small minded and jealous of you.

Don't Expect Them To Help You

You cannot expect people to be there for you like you're there for them because they are not you, and besides, if you're always bailing someone out of tough situations, it's because they have poor judgement, so how could you expect them to be there for you when you're in need of help.

When to Discuss Heated Topics

Never try to resolve a problem with a hotheaded person while they are in defense mode. They are not listening to understand, they are looking for you to stop talking so they can reply. Before you speak, listen; before you react, think; before you criticize, gather the facts.

Let Go Of The Dead Weight

So often, we let great opportunities pass us by because we are holding onto something we should have let go. To move on, you have to let go of things that are holding you down.

Can You Afford It?

Don't spend money you don't have to buy things you don't need just to impress people. Always live within your means, don't spend more than you need to or have to. If the item in question is not going to help you get a job, a promotion, or bring in extra income, it's not worth it.

Turn The Page or Close The Book

It can be a relationship, friendship or job. You must decide if you are going to stay or walk away from it, regardless of the amount of time, energy, or money you have invested. You must weigh the pros and cons; either fix the issue or leave.

Sometimes No Reaction Is The Best Reaction

Never speak when you're angry because your mouth is moving faster than your mind. Depending on the situation, you may want to give no response, process the situation and provide a response or act on it later.

Expect Nothing In Return

Expect nothing from other people in return when you do a kind act, and you will appreciate anything they give. Don't expect people to do the same for you as you do for them; not everyone has the same heart as you.

Dealing With Rude People

If it is on the job or off the job, if you have no choice but to interact with someone that has a nasty attitude, always remember that person can be going through something tough and one kind word or interaction can change the person's entire day. So try and be the bigger person.

They Don't Want To Be Saved

Sometimes you have to give up on a person you love not because you don't care about them anymore, but because they don't care about themselves enough to want to change.

Stop Going With The Flow

Life is not a game, it's serious business, and if you don't spend time overanalyzing, overthinking, and overreacting to life, you will get left behind.

Look At The Reward—Not The Work

When you survive or overcome a major problem in your life, don't look back at the stress you endured. Instead, realize how much strength you now have because you overcame that problem.

Focus on the Opportunity—Not the Obligation

Every opportunity comes with specific obligations; you must always concentrate on the opportunity, not the obligation. Nothing great comes for free and without hard work.

A Bad Attitude Gets You Nowhere

Having a bad attitude would normally get you nowhere fast. In your personal life, you will have very little or no friends. In your career, you will not advance, and you more than likely will end up old and alone.

Don't Be A Know It All

A moron will always be a fool because they think they know everything. Therefore, they don't need to learn anything new. Always keep your mind open to new ideas because no matter how smart you are on a subject, you don't know everything.

You Have To Start Somewhere

You may have all the degrees in the world and be more experienced than your boss, but when you start a new job, you have to start somewhere. There's only one job that you start off at the top, and that's when you're digging a hole. Remember to get ahead in life. You have to start somewhere.

You've Had Worse Days

So you woke up late, got stuck in traffic, walked into a mess at work, and you forgot your presentation at home. Always remember today may be a bad day, but you've had worse days; you may wake up with some aches and pains, but you woke up. Your life may not be perfect, but you're better off than some. Happiness comes when you stop complaining about the troubles you have, and you're thankful for all the problems you don't have.

Your Needs Versus Wants

Too often people focus on wants that they don't have, and not on the fact that all their needs are not fulfilled. Forget the wants if you don't have what you need.

People That Gossip

Gossip dies when it meets the ears of a wise person; it's said that below-average people talk about people who make things happen, average people talk about what's happening, wise people make things happen.

Only Speak When It's Needed

It can be at work or in your personal life, but you should never enter a conversation unless you have something of value to add. A smart person knows when to speak and when not to.

Do What You Love

You know you are working your dream job when you leave home early, stay at work late and have no complaints about doing it. If you do what you love, you'll never work a day in your life. Passion is the difference between having a career and having a job. Figure out what you like to do and get somebody to pay you to do it.

People Will Always Have Something to Say

You shouldn't get upset or discouraged because no matter what you do—good or bad—people will always have something negative to say. You just can't please everyone, so don't let the behavior of others destroy your character. The less you respond to negativity, the more peaceful your life will become.

I Love You But Bye

You can't control who you fall in love with, but just because you love them, if they begin to drag you down, you must know when to cut them loose. It's okay for someone to stay in your heart but not in your life. You can't reach for something new if you're holding on to yesterday's junk. Walk away from anything that no longer serves its purpose, grows you, or makes you happy. Just because you love someone doesn't mean you're supposed to be with them.

How To Look At Life

Hope for the best but prepare for the worst. Learn from yesterday; live for today; hope for tomorrow.

Forgive To Move Forward

When you're upset, you can't think straight, your mind can't focus, so you must forgive or come to terms with who or whatever is creating your anger. You don't forgive others to be kind; you forgive others for you to move forward.

You're What You Think About

You are and will become what you think of all day, so if you spend your days thinking of nothing, you will become nothing.

Complaining Is Wasting Time

Why waste time complaining about something that has already happened when you should focus on fixing the problem. Spending today complaining about yesterday will not make tomorrow any better.

What Is It To Love Someone

For some people, they truly believe if they love someone, then that means they should be together. But the truth is if you love someone, you want them to be happy—even if it's not with you. Love is caring for each other even when you're angry.

Character Versus Talent

Many celebrities lose tons of money or throw away their careers because of their actions. Their talent can take them places; their character won't be able to keep them. No matter how talented you are, your character can always destroy anything your talent built.

We All Need Someone At One Point

You shouldn't depend on others, but there will be a time when you need the help of others. Be robust enough to stand alone, but be wise enough to stand with others when the time comes.

Knowing What And How To Say It

Everyone wants to get their point across when interacting with others. The key thing to remember is it's not what you say, but how you say it that determines the direction of the interaction. Knowledge is knowing what to say; wisdom is knowing when and how to say it.

How Low Are You Aiming

Having a goal in life is important, and what I see is that some people fail in life not because they set their goals too high and miss, but because they set their goals too low, and they hit it. Remember a goal is what you want it to be, but make sure you are not setting your goals based on lack of belief in yourself.

Stop Planting Your Own Fears

Don't spend too much time worrying about something that has never happened or you will trick yourself into believing it has happened, it's happening, or it's going to happen.

Prepare For What's Next

People that live in the moment are often the ones whose future is in disarray. You must learn to enjoy today, but be prepared for tomorrow.

Why The Same Problems Keep Happening

When a situation happens that you like or dislike, you must evaluate the cause of the situation if you wish to prevent it from happening again. Next time handle that situation differently. Remember, the things that happen in life should be viewed as a lesson. Life lessons will continuously be repeated until you learn from them. You cannot solve a problem with the same thinking that created the problem.

Difference Between A Mistake And A Choice

When a mistake is made for the first time, you should look at it as a lesson so that you don't repeat it twice. When you mess-up the first time, it's a mistake, the second time you make that same mistake it's by choice. You chose not to be smart and learn from your mistake.

Get All The Facts Before You Have An Opinion

Don't speak on something you don't fully understand; too many people have full opinions, but only half the facts. Every day, stand guard at the gates of your mind. Don't be influenced by others' negative thinking. Always make sure your opinion is a product of your research; don't let it be the result of someone else's thinking.

The Best Type of Revenge

When someone tries or has hurt you, the best revenge you can have is to become successful. That will show them what they thought they did to hurt you, really had no effect on you.

Remember Them For What They Are Now

When it comes to relationships, family, or friends, we can't be stuck on the fact that they were once a nice person if they're now a jerk. You must see things for what they now are, not what they use to be. We're often blind to the present because we are so focused on the past. Don't be afraid of change; you may lose something bad to gain something better.

Be Grateful For What You Got

Stop hating yourself for not being rich, for not having a nice car, for not having a great job. Start loving yourself and be grateful for what you have—no matter how little it may be—because you can always gain more if you focus on the solution instead of the problem.

Don't Change For People You Don't Like

Look at how you act, dress or talk. Are you doing these things to impress people you don't care to be around or even like?

Use The Tools You Have

When working toward your goal, don't focus on tools or resources you should have but don't have. Instead, concentrate on the tools or resources in front of you.

Choose Your Friends Carefully

Take a moment to look at the people you spend the most time with. Do you want to be like them? The chances are you will become like the five people you spend the most time around.

It's Not Real, Time To Let Go

Sometimes we may fall for a lie, and that's ok; no one is perfect, but the moment you realize it is a lie, you have to be willing to let go, no matter how much you believed in it. One of the hardest things in life is letting go what you thought was real.

The Argument You Will Always Lose

Never argue with an idiot. To the idiot, common sense and facts don't matter. You can make all the sense in the world, have the facts laid out in front of the person, and still, they will refuse to accept or understand the truth.

Never Lend Money You Can't Afford To Lose

Friends and family will always require some form of financial assistance, and if you wish to keep that person in your life, never lend them money you can't afford to lose. If that friend or family is already in a financial hole, the funds you provide may not be enough to get them out of that hole and back on their feet to the point that they can pay you back.

The Truth Hurts But It's Better Than Lying

You should tell the truth to people you care about and love—no matter how much it may hurt them. Telling the truth and making someone cry is better than telling a lie so they can smile, then walk out the door and look like a fool. I would rather hear that what am doing, saying, or how am behaving is like a fool, from a loved one, rather than make a fool of myself in public.

How To Destroy Trust

It can be in your personal, professional, or love life. You do not have a one hundred percent trust in someone you just met. It takes some time to build that trust. You can spend years building trust, and one act or wrong decision can destroy that trust, and do you know why? It's because you expected that person to know better and they should have done better.

They Are Jealous Because They Aren't You

People are often jealous because you have something they want but don't have. So pay attention to the people around you and remember you can't be friends with someone who wants your life. They're just waiting for the chance to push you down and take over your life.

Don't Be With Someone If You Can't Be Yourself

Who do you want to be? Is that person allowing you to be what you want to be? Will that person stay once you become or show what you want to be? Is that person helping you become what you want yourself to be? If your answer is "No" or "I don't know"—you need to leave or find out the answer.

Let Your Actions Speak For You

Not everyone should get an explanation. Some people only hear what they want to hear. Right or wrong, people will always think or assume things about you, but only *your* actions can confirm or deny their assumptions.

How To Meet The Right Person

Be the type of person you want to meet. If you want a caring, smart, and responsible partner, start by being a caring, intelligent, and accountable person. By doing that, you will end up around caring, smart, and capable people.

They're Dead; They Had It Coming

It's called having respect for the dead, but what if the dead was a killer or rapist? Are we not to talk ill of the dead because they are dead? Just because someone is dead doesn't mean they weren't a jerk in life or deserved to die. As the old saying goes, you live by the sword, so you die by the sword. If you are caught committing a crime, and in the process, you're killed due to your actions. Oh well, have a nice afterlife. Why lose sleep over something you already knew would be the outcome. I remember hearing a mother say, "I can still remember the call I got that night telling me my son was dead. He was shot in the process of robbing some store. Ever since that night, I have slept like a baby, because I know exactly where he is every night now, and I don't have to worry about getting that call anymore." She knew what kind of a lifestyle her son lived, and she knew that he would most likely die due to his way of life.

Are You Single, Or You Think You're Single

If you have a problem that affects you, and your partner chooses not to be involved with the solution process, then you're single. If you have an issue that affects you, and you don't tell your partner because you don't want them involved, then you think you're single. When you're in a relationship, your actions not only affect you, but they also affect your partner. You both are a team now, and there is no "I" in a team.

A Partner's Support

No, I do not believe in: "If you love me you, should accept me for who I am." If a person's goal and vision for the future is going to hinder you from reaching yours, then maybe you shouldn't be together. In a relationship, your partner should accept your past, but you must be honest and upfront about the history, not three plus years into the relationship. Your partner should support your present if it is in line with what you both have planned for the future, and your partner should encourage your future.

There Is A Time And Place for Everything

Depending on your job and position, there are rules of conduct you must follow. When you are in a relationship, there are certain expectations your partner has of you. As a parent, you must be a good example for your children. When with friends, you can let your hair down and just be yourself. We all have different hats we must wear. Be sure to wear the right one at the right time. When with your kids, you should have your parent hat—not your "having drinks with friend's hat" talking about what you did last night.

You've Got to Believe In What You Do

Sometimes you don't need a plan B because it distracts you from plan A. If you're going to do something, do what you believe in and do it to the best of your ability. Why waste time or money doing something you don't believe in? Three things you must remember: know what you're doing, love what you're doing, and believe in what you're doing.

How Valuable Are You?

Take a moment and think about your job. If you walked into your boss's office and told them that you're giving your two-week notice, would they offer you a raise or promotion to stay? If you know that they would say: "Sorry to see you leave but good luck." Then maybe the problem is that you have not made yourself so valuable to your company that you have become indispensable.

Just Keep Moving

Everyone moves at their own pace, it can be your career, in your relationships, or working on a goal. It doesn't matter how slow you move, as long as you don't stop moving forward.

Life Is Not Finding Yourself

You're not lost; life is about creating yourself and developing your character based on your life experiences.

Small Things Add Up to Big Things

When working on anything including yourself, you can start off small. Little tweaks here and there add up to big changes, once you take a step back to look at the overall big picture, you'll notice the changes.

Become a Leader at What You Do

No matter what industry you work in, become such an expert at what you do, you no longer must introduce yourself when you meet others from your industry. They will already know who you are.

They Won't Always Understand

Your dreams and goals are yours and yours alone to know. It's okay to live a life others will not understand because they do not have the vision you have.

Quit—and You'll Be Working for a Winner

People that stopped too soon or never tried to reach their goals are employed by the people that never gave up on their goals.

Leaders Create Other Leaders

A leader is a teacher, trainer, and protector. You can measure yourself as a leader by the number of leaders you've inspired.

Your Weird Is Someone's Normal

Every person is unique and plays a special role in this world. Each person is different in their way, so don't pass judgment; what's weird for you may be normal for someone else. So respect each other's beliefs and point of view.

Make a Living But Have A Life

You should have goals, and you should work hard to reach them. Just don't get so busy making a living that you forget to have a life. That's one way to gain everything you want and lose everything you need. You can have all the money you desire, but without someone or family to share it with, then what good is the money.

You Don't Need To Be An Expert

You don't need to know everything to get something done, just surround yourself with people who know a little bit of everything you want to get done.

Friends That Report Gossip

Don't tell me what was said about me; tell me why they were so comfortable to say it to you or in front of you?

Straightforward People

Direct people are typically real friends; they agree with you when you're right and tell you when you're wrong. Unfortunately, everyone can't deal with the truth, so you will notice a lot of honest people have few friends.

Don't Be A Hypocrite

People are quick to judge others, but if they took a moment and looked at their actions, they would notice how they're doing the same things, they talk down to someone else for doing. It's weird how when someone else does something, it's wrong, but when they do it, it's ok. Don't be or do what you hate other people for being or doing. Don't be a hypocrite.

We Assign The Word "Friends" Too Freely

To be a friend, you must have a history together; they must have been there through the tough times. If you work together; you're co-workers. If you go to school together; you're classmates. If you live together; you're roommates. Just because you know someone's name and hang out once in a while doesn't make them a friend.

Something Is Better Than Nothing

You cannot concern yourself with what other people have if they make a dollar and you make fifty cents doing the same thing. You should speak up or find a better deal, but don't just walk away and have nothing lined up. A little bit of something is better than all of nothing.

You Can't Ignore The Truth

Acknowledge that the situation is bad, but now you must find a solution to the situation. You can close your eyes to things you don't want to see, but they will still be there, so confront it head on.

How The Rich Got Rich

If you think about it, every wealthy person provides a valuable service. The person whose service provides the most value typically becomes rich. What service will you provide?

Rules/Morals To Live By

1. Never underestimate anyone or anything. Always act as if you are going up against your most challenging situation. This way, you are over prepared and focused on the task at hand in front of you. Remember, the story of the tortoise and the hare; the hare figured that the tortoise was so slow and took a nap in the middle of the race, and by the time he woke up, the tortoise was at the finish line and won the race.

2. Don't cry wolf, in other words, don't say something has happened or is going to happen because one of two things will happen. One, the thing you believe will happen or are saying has happened will one day happen and no one will believe you. Two, you will have said the situation has happened or will happen so much that you will convince yourself the situation has happened or will actually happen.

3. There's a time to work, and there's a time to play. If you are playing around when you should be working, studying, listening, or learning, you will always be a few steps behind, and the people that are doing what they are supposed to do are the ones that are always a few steps ahead.

4. Work smart—not hard. When you approach anything in life, think what would be the simplest and easiest solution. This way, you do not overwork yourself or start to become overwhelmed by the task at hand.

5. Don't be a fool. Use common sense. Look at the situation, take what you know about the situation, and apply the information you gathered to find a solution

6. Be honest and trustworthy; there is an old saying: "The best way to judge a person's character is not by what they do when people are around, but by what they do when people are not around." It is not ok to do something just because no one is around to catch you.

7. Whenever you can, help someone who needs it; it can be a significant gesture or a little gesture—just help someone whenever you can. Always remember you will come across those who you will help, and they will not appreciate what you've done, but you must remember them the next time they are in need of help. At that time, don't help them. Why help someone who is ungrateful or doesn't want to help themselve?

8. Be humble; be smart enough to know what you know and don't know. There will always be someone better at something than you. If your head gets too big, no one will want to be around you.

9. Want more but appreciate what little you have—because some people don't have anything.

10. Everyone needs someone; no one can do everything on their own all the time.

11. Only be a true friend to someone else that is a true friend to you. Not everyone you associate with is a friend.

12. Don't be surprised when someone does something that's only a natural part of their character. Thieves steal, and liars lie.

13. The amount of money you have does not determine your success. Your happiness with life determines your success. Many rich people are so unhappy with their lives that they kill themselves.

14. Don't let bad habits become habits. If you realize you do certain things that you don't like, address the issue and fix it before it becomes part of your character.

15. Control your temper. If you get heated about a situation, you should step back and revisit it after you have cooled down.

16. Don't judge a book by its cover; always gather your facts before you base a judgment on someone else's words.

Everyday Issues We Face

Money problems.

Not having enough to cover all your basic expense; look at all your expense and cut out any unnecessary overhead.

Credit card debt.

Owe more money than you can afford to pay back, which is holding you back from reaching your goal. Cut up your cards and start paying down your bills.

Parents who don't understand us.

Some parents just don't understand, but a majority of them do and want the best for us; the problem is we don't want to listen.

Friends who don't support us.

You've got two types of friends the ones that are fake friends, actual undercover haters; they will never support you. Then you have real friends; the ones who are not supporting you because you're headed down the wrong path.

Having rent to pay every month.

If you are complaining about rent, then move back home and stay with your parents and live by their rules. Paying rent or a mortgage is part of being an adult, so deal with it.

Hating our job.

It's only natural that you hate your job. You should never be working a job, you should be working at your career. Also, you only hate your job if it's not helping you work towards your career.

Being unable to find a better job.

Stop looking for a job, start looking for a career, and when you are called in for an interview, research the company. Find out what issues or problems they have, and at your interview, you tell them what possible solutions you have to offer them.

Deciding whether or not to go back to school.

Not every career requires a degree, but if you choose to revisit school, make sure you pick a degree based on your career path.

Trying to stay trendy.

Being trendy is pointless... and expensive. Unless you're a public figure, it doesn't matter.

Not knowing what's going on in the world.

You don't have to know everything, but you should be well-informed of your industry.

Finding a soulmate.

You first have to know who you are, what you want, where you're going, and your relationship expectations before you start looking for a soulmate. The worst thing you can do is find the right person and lose them because you weren't ready.

Not knowing ourselves well enough.

You must know your bad habits. (We all have them.) This way, when someone points them out, you won't get mad.

Thinking we know it all.

Not understanding that in the grand scheme of things, we don't know anything. So always be willing to listen and learn from those who have something to teach.

Spending too much time on Facebook or social media.

Unless you are marketing or making money on social media, you shouldn't spend too much time on it. Sometimes you get so caught up in seeing what's going on in other people's lives you don't pay attention to your own life as it falls apart in front of you.

Not getting enough exercise.

Depending on your goals or lifestyle, being healthy may play a huge role.

Pulling an all-nighter and then regretting it in the morning.

Unless pulling an all-nighter is helping you get closer to achieving your goal, you just wasted valuable time you could have used to recharge your battery.

Deciding which tattoo to get — aka which one you'll regret the most in twenty years.

Remember you will get old, and that tattoo of a red cherry will turn into an apple one day.

Not listening to others.

It's ok to seek advice; just don't look or take advice from someone in the same situation, who is unable to get out of it themselves.

Feeling privileged.

People that love you, do for you because they love you, not because they have to. So be grateful that they love you and are willing to do for you.

Being unable to empathize.

Before you judge or act, try putting yourself in that person's shoes and think how you would feel if it happened to you.

Using sympathy as a way to insult people.

Teasing is bad but using sympathy is one of the lowest forms of teasing.

Being opinionated on subjects you know nothing about.

Before you speak on any subject, make sure you know what you're talking about; don't refer to hearsay. Have the facts or keep quiet.

Trolling everyone who speaks their mind.

You may not agree with someone's point of view, but as long as they are not hurting anyone, leave them be.

Watching reality TV (while ignoring reality).

You are what you watch; keep watching the crazy housewives, and you'll find yourself becoming a crazy housewife.

Complaining about everything and anything.

This is typically a miserable person who can be happy but does not want to be satisfied with anything. Stay away from this type of person.

Being too picky.

It's okay to be picky, as long as you're willing to live up to the same standards you set for others.

Being too stubborn.

You must be open to change and other people's point of view—otherwise you will never grow.

Being close-minded, but thinking you're open-minded.

This is called lying to yourself, and at the end of the day, only you can see or correct that issue. (Most people like this know that they are lying to themselves.)

Having to tell a partner it's not going to work out.

Unless you're a really good actor, your partner should be able to see it coming from a mile away. Just be honest and tell them you don't think it's going to work.

Bringing the wrong people into your life...Allowing those wrong people to remain part of your life.

This will only bring you drama.

Allowing others to make decisions for you.

No one already knows what you truly want and can handle except you.

Not speaking up.

You will always end up with the short end of the stick if you stay silent on things that will affect you.

Being afraid of greatness.

You will not live to your full potential.

Acting like we're better than others.

Quick way to end up hurt or in deep trouble, you've got to be humble. You may be good at something, but there's always someone better.

Being too proud to ask for help when we need it.

You will get stuck at some point in life, so don't let your pride prevent you from asking for help.

Not being considerate of others; thinking the world revolves around you.

You will end up with no friends.

Lying for the hell of it.

No one will trust you.

Sleeping with all the wrong people.

You can end up with an STD or a bad reputation, which can cause you to miss out on the right person.

Not being able to find a suitable mentor or role model.

You will follow fools who will lead you nowhere.

Not being in love with learning.

You will not grow or advance much in life.

Thinking "YOLO" is how you should live.

You will live a high speed but unaccomplished life.

Allowing yourself to be wounded by careless, hurtful people and expecting them to change their ways.

You're wasting time.

Not accepting the fact that manipulation is important if we wish to succeed.

In the real world, you have to deal with the fact that things are not fair and you must play the game in order to get ahead.

Spending your time foolishly.

Anything you do should be adding value to your life.

Never slowing down...because we're afraid life itself is boring.

Those quite boring moments are what you use to reflect on your life.

Not traveling enough and experiencing other cultures.

You will limit your understanding of the world.

Not giving a damn — about anything.

You will do anything without thought, landing you in a lot of trouble.

Bullying people. We all do it, even if we don't realize it.

What goes around comes around.

Not saving money because we think there is no way we can.

Take a good look at your finances. What extras can you get rid of?

Forgetting about the concept of courtship.

You will find yourself with someone you hate.

Doing things without a purpose.

You will waste time and find yourself moving backward, or at a standstill.

Not thinking before acting.

You will have many regrets.

Not spending more time with your family.

When problems come, you will feel alone and as if you have no one to turn to.

Not telling those that we love, that we love them; not appreciating the individuals who are most important in our lives.

We will lose them.

Not appreciating the little things.

We will never see the big picture.

Giving up on dreams when the going gets tough.

Life is not meant to be easy. The harder the fight. the greater the reward.

Being very good at coming up with excuses.

You will never accept blame for anything you do.

Being too overloaded with unimportant information to remember the important things.

If you don't prioritize things, your life will fall apart.

Not talking when you have problems.

Communication is one of the most important things you can do if you want to resolve a problem.

Thinking there will always be a tomorrow.

Based on the situation, you must act in the moment if needed, because tomorrow is not guaranteed.

Not spending every hour of every day improving yourself, making yourself better, stronger, smarter.

You will not grow.

Conclusion

Your goals are whatever makes you happy, and being a success at your goal is working towards it; you don't have to accomplish it, but you should be actively working towards that goal. Your goal is like the fuel that drives you in life, and when you die, you want to make sure that you died on E (empty). You want to make sure that you've gone out there: you've accomplished or worked on every single goal you've ever had. You don't want to die not living a fulfilling life. When you die and leave this earth, how many people will show up at your funeral? How many lives will you have touched? What legacy will you leave behind? And it's not necessarily a legacy that you would leave behind for the world, but for the people closest to you, for the people that your goals will affect. How many of them will mourn your loss?

Remember, never stop wanting more. Your imagination can take you a lot further than your logic can. No matter how bad or how desperate the situation may seem, never stop working toward your goal. No matter what people say about your ideas, never stop working at your goal. Don't switch from imagination mode to logic mode because your logic will tell you that your goals are not possible. You will never be ready, and you will never know when you are ready to get started on your goals. The question is, are you willing to put in the hard work? Are you willing to be focused? And are you willing to walk away from things that hold you back? Are you ready to deal with all the people who will doubt you? Are you willing to deal with all of the sacrifices before you succeed? Are you willing to give up the things you thought were important? If you're willing to take on every challenge that comes your way, then go for it.

Everybody has a desire to do something, but you must have discipline and dedication to that goal; things are not going to happen when you want them to happen. There's a process for everything. Your goal is going to be difficult, and the key thing is not to see the work you have to put in to accomplish your goal as an obligation. But look at it in small parts. It's similar to building a wall. You never look at the entire length and height that you have to build the wall because you start to tell yourself it's too much work it's too hard. What you must do is lay down your first brick, then the second and third and fourth, and before you know it, you've accomplished what you set out to do. You've built a wall. Working toward your goal is not going to be easy, and it is not supposed to be easy. Just work at it one step at a time.

You cannot expect or want the convenience of succeeding at your goal without the associated inconvenience of the hard work or obstacles.

Without realizing it, the small decisions that we make every day can keep us on track to our goals or divert us in a whole other direction. Small decisions, such as not to get up on time, not to eat the right things, not to be an angry person that just snaps for no reason, the decision not to speak up when you know that somebody did wrong. The decision not to look for a better job and just complain about the one that you have now. Then one day you wake up, you look at your life, and you are like, "What the heck happened? How did I end up in such an unfortunate predicament?"

No matter who it is, if that person has done something to better themselves whether financially, emotionally, or personally, they had to overcome some form of an obstacle; there is no easy road, it does not exist. If you find yourself making an excuse as to why you have not succeeded in life, the truth of the matter is you simply are not willing to overcome those obstacles that are keeping you from achieving your goal. When working towards your goal, the obstacles that you overcome help to build your character. See the obstacle, understand the barrier, and do it anyway. Yes, you will fall but you will learn from your mistakes, and you will improve to become better.

What are your ethics? What is the moral code that you live by? What are the lines that you will not cross to become successful? You must have them established. You must live by those values. This way, once you accomplish your goal, you'll be able to sleep at night to wake up in the morning and look at yourself in the mirror.

Accept the real world for what it is. Don't live in a fantasyland where you expect what's right is right and what's wrong is wrong. It is not like that. There are some of us that have real disadvantages, but we cannot use them as crutches; we shouldn't use them as excuses.

You will have to deal with people you don't like; you will have to laugh at jokes that are not funny; you will have to go to dinner with people you can't stand, but that is the reality of life, that is the reality that we currently live. We may not like the people we do business with; we may not like the people we meet on a path to our goals, but if those very same people can help you accomplish or reach your goals, you must be ready and willing to work with them. Do not let your pride and ego get out of control and kill the opportunities; you have to succeed at your goal. Things will happen in life that will require you to put your goals on hold, and that's okay. Just be sure that they are real issues and not issues you made up.

The worst thing anyone can do after reading this book is to have the knowledge to know better and not do better. Now that you know better, the question is, are you going to do better?

Don't lie to yourself if you know you're not working as hard as you should be working towards a goal and you're destroying relationships because you cannot accept your friends and loved ones telling you the truth.

You cannot have tunnel vision and only see the things that you want to see; it is better to get the point of view of the person standing outside the window looking in.

You cannot be a lazy, unprofessional person, having a horrible attitude. When things don't go your way, you shouldn't find a way to blame everyone else and fail to acknowledge the things you have done to contribute to the situation not working out the way you would like.

Final Thought

I remember listening to Earl Nightingale's "The Strangest Secret"—originally published in 1976. Even then, he talked about us living in the Golden Era, especially here in the United States and how we have access to an abundant amount of education, riches, and opportunity for everyone. If you ask a child what they want to be when they grow up? They'll say that they want to be successful. They'll pick careers that reflect that: a doctor, lawyer, or teacher. No one's going to say, "I want to be a bum; I want to be out on the streets; I want to depend on my family and the government to take care of me." All kids have to go through the same level of education starting at pre-k; all the way up to high school they all have the same educational opportunity. Therefore, they have the same opportunity to succeed or fail in life. We, as parents, are the ones who decide directly or indirectly who or what will influence the thinking habits of our kids. For example, if you sit your child in front of the television for a good period during the day on a kid friendly channel like Disney or Cartoon Network, your child will want a kid meal from McDonalds or Burger King; they will know the latest toys and want to watch the newest kid movie in the theaters. Because that is what the advertisers on Disney and Cartoon Network are programming your child to want. My point is, we are sponges from the time we are born. We are influenced by the people and circumstances around us. It's not your fault; it's just something that we have inherently done from the time we were kids. We conform to fit into our environment. In school, we want to be liked by everyone, so what do we do? We start to act and talk like everyone else to fit in; we do this year after year, grade after grade, and by the time we graduate high school, we are essentially a carbon copy of every other student at that school. We have adapted our mindset and ideologies to fit the crowd, for good or bad, only time will tell.

You will never become who you want to be if you are too attached to who you've been, and you hear it all the time, people say, "Well, I've always been this way." If you're happy with the outcome of your life, keep doing what you're doing. If you're not happy with your current life situation, then change what you've been doing.

To Book Author for Speaking Engagements:

To Book author for speaking engagements with corporations, associations, or other organizations. Contact the publisher at the website below.

www.adleytelfort.com

E-mail: bookings@adleytelfort.com

Notes

www.ingramcontent.com/pod-product-compliance
Lightning Source LLC
Chambersburg PA
CBHW072158090426
42740CB00012B/2315